I0334840

CLIMBING A DELICATE SCAFFOLDING

TRICIA YOST

Radial Books

Also by Tricia Yost
First Things
Votives: Entries from the Daybooks of Gertrude Tate, 1898-1952
Factory
Youth At Risk
All That Is Behind Us Now

Copyright © 2024 by Tricia Yost
All rights reserved.

The poems in this book though they may reference historical events, real locations, and/or real people, are fictitious.

No part of this publication may be reproduced, distributed, or transmitted in any form or by any means, without the prior written permission of the publisher.

Published by Radial Books
radialbooks.org

Climbing a Delicate Scaffolding/ Tricia Yost, 1st ed.

ISBN: 978-0-9984146-8-3

Cover Art: *First Light*, Annette Lusher, 2021.

ACKNOWLEDGMENTS

The poems in this book first appeared, sometimes in slightly different forms, in *Cream City Review, String Town, Parnassus Literary Journal, Smartish Pace, Borderlands, The Adirondack Review, Crack the Spine, Crab Fat Magazine,* and *Center*. Grateful acknowledgment is made to the editors of these journals.

Grateful acknowledgment as always to Kent Fielding and Ryan Masters for their close reading and feedback.

When it's this windy doesn't it seem impossible to grow
old?

OLENA KALYTIAK DAVIS from *And Her Soul Out of Nothing*

It is the pace of our living that makes the world available.

JACK GILBERT from *Refusing Heaven*

CONTENTS

A GARAGE IN OHIO 1
SMALL TOWN GIRL SEIZES THE DAY 3
ALL THE CIGARETTES TO COME 4
ETERNITY 6
THE RECKLESS ABOUT HER 8
AVERAGE 11
DANIEL 12
WHEN HER BROTHERS WERE BOYS 13
NORTHERN LIGHTS, FAIRBANKS, ALASKA 15
STAGES 16
IN THE MIDWEST EVERYONE IS KIND 18
NOSH 19
OF ALL THE MARVELOUS THINGS 20
MADD RIVER, OHIO 22
RESOLUTION 23
TREADING 25
PORTRAIT OF THE UNSPOKEN 26
PLEASURES 29
WHAT HAS HAPPENED 30
THE ART OF FLYING 31
NOTES TOWARD FLIGHT 33
HERE 34
DANIEL 35
TAG 36

QUANTUM THEORY	37
MIDLIFE	38
SYLVIA HOTEL	39
JUG'S TAVERN	40
HER MOTHER AND A MAN	42
THEATER ON DIVISION STREET	44
PARTICIPLING	46
TAKING DOWN THE PLANE	47
YOU DON'T NEED TO CATCH A THING	48
ON FINDING SHE WAKES EARLIER AS SHE GETS OLDER	49
THE NEW CHRONOLOGY	50
EVERYTHING TO LOOK FORWARD TO	51
DEAD LETTER OFFICE	52
AS SUMMER ENDS	54
PALIMPSEST	56
AS LONG AS YOU'RE HERE	57
THE BURDEN OF THE OPEN ROAD	58

A GARAGE IN OHIO

As a young girl she followed
at her father's heels and watched him
gather with his brothers in the garage
around a pristine red '67 Chevy.
Cherry red, someone said.
What a beaut. Its hood angling
toward heaven and the belly hollowed clean,
absent of twisting metal. The men
congregated as if around a sacred shroud.
They held their cans of Hamm's
Uncle Roy said, *Not gonna matter*
the body ain't got a scratch on it
'less you get something strong going
beneath the hood. He was the only one
without a beer and curled his thumbs
in the loops of his Levis, his fingers
dangling. He was the oldest and so
the wisest. He'd been to war
and come back. Her father didn't
care what he had to say, like he didn't care
for what his father was always saying:
Fast cars won't get you anywhere.
What you need is a job. A union job.
Jeep's hiring. I can get you in.
The factory wasn't for her father,
assembling the same parts all day.
He wanted a car on his own terms,
built from nothing but an idea in his head.
So what if after two years of greased
knuckles, hundreds of dollars, so what
if after all that time alone,
the car didn't run, and he sold the frame
to a junkyard dealer, she had peered
into the gaping hole, and though she didn't

understand what drew him
to the red shell, in the dusty,
sun-smoked garage she saw his eyes.
They said, *Just wait. You'll see.*

SMALL TOWN GIRL SEIZES THE DAY

There's a girl who doesn't yet know
she has will. Her life is a series of rituals:
Sundays, the dry host and her warm mouth,
crossing and kneeling and praying. She prays her house
won't catch fire, that her father will find a job, for an A in algebra.
The devotions come without thought.
She has learned the necessary gestures. Has been told
she is good. How could she be otherwise? At that age
appearances are everything and the very young mean to please.

In four years that girl will take a boy from behind because she
won't get pregnant, but still means to please. Her own pleasure is
learning to be tied to this. It becomes a Saturday night ritual after
talk and a movie with friends. Soon she'll seek pain because pain
suggests she's real. Pain, close cousin to pleasure.
The impulse toward drugs or the adrenaline rush, fear factor
of jumping forty-five feet from a railroad bridge into river waters
of unknown depth will grow, will push through her body, because
it's through the body, not through a dead God, that one comes to
know.

ALL THE CIGARETTES TO COME

There is no particular one she misses.
Not the morning burn
that complements dark coffee.
Not the hurried late afternoon break
from work, outside near the awning
as rain comes down, slowing everything
down for those few minutes.

Nor that first one, firm Winston
slid from her father's pack into her own back
pocket. The illicit hold. Scraping the wooden
match against the garage's green shingle.
Or any summer night, when she was
sixteen and blew smoke at the Ohio's fat moon.

The ones she wants are the ones to come:
The plane lands and she's out
in the chilly air, catching
a light from a stranger who has stubbed his
and is heading in, leaving her
to quick pulls and breezy exhales
as she kicks at the firm ground beneath her feet.

Or at two a.m. when her lover,
showered, robed, joins her on the back
stoop as her parted lips pucker
around a filter. She sparks the night,
and exhales wearily until the quiet gray streak
thins into a line of nothingness.

If she sits long enough, she'll remember
and maybe long for those stubs
plucked from ceramic trays found in every corner,

she'll remember her young cheeks caving
toward the lipsticked ends, nicotine threading,
inciting the buds on her young tongue,
brief glimpses of all the cigarettes to come.

ETERNITY

She has never had to talk anyone down
off a bad trip or talk anyone
into giving her the gun.
She has never had to talk
anyone out of suicide
except herself, which seemed silly,
talking with such gravity
when she knew she wasn't really
going to.
It's that hour of night
when anyone
will do anything
not to be alone.
All day she has been trying
to get back to sleep.
Trying to get back
to that warm dream
where sunlight was.
Five years ago,
she would have dropped a blotter
and walked on water
in the neighbor's pool or felt
the thrust of a fist inside her
and been happy.
It's that hour
when it's too late to bother
to sleep
and too early to start the day.
That hour when cats fight
between garages and books
have gone cold. The hour
of lamenting youth
and foolish things, when she wants the ease

after a few drinks
or a certain woman
who is fiercely attracted to men,
that hour when raccoons
root through the garbage
causing her to wonder what part of her
is that interesting.
It's that hour when bars are closed
but if they weren't she'd find a man
to take home after ten years
of being with women.
It's that hour
when grief weighs so much
that she wants out from under its yoke
despite knowing her life is good, safe,
except for this hour, this endless hour
thinking of the hours without

THE RECKLESS ABOUT HER

Summer days she rode bikes with boys
in Toledo neighborhoods, laughing
at shorn lawns and sculptured hedges
of Ottawa Hills, ditching soda cans
in the driveways of mansions
or trailing mud and tire-tracks
in the open backyards of houses
in Sylvania, sometimes unknowingly
crossing the line into the low-rolling
hills of Michigan, but always returning
home to careen down Langenderfer,
the one smooth one-way street,
fast in its long panes of concrete.
Its west end curving away
from the highway and back into tracts
of middle-class brick.
Across from those was Drummond Park
where stray kids hung from net-less rims,
twisting them useless
where swing-sets and merry-go-rounds
rusted after the briefest rain.
Through a break in the chain-link
she'd cut behind the bowling alley, its walls
blistering old paint and the lot
smattered with brown glass,
she'd lose the sun in a grove of fir,
blink back dust from the trails of dirt hills
the boys had spent hours pushing around.
The boys caught air, kicked their legs,
and came down hard on the pedals
or crashed to their knees.
She watched their speed,
their rising to futile heights.

She tried to follow
the driveway curbs
and dirt hills and catch a lift
that she could handle.

WHEN WE THINK OF THE FUTURE THE PAST COMES TO MIND

In the bucket seat of her father's hand-fused buggy,
the ragtop unsnapped and left home,
wind whips between the seats, bandies her father's shirtsleeves
and the loose threads of her short pants. Ten and tucked
in a wool blanket, drifting out and in to a sleep
edged with an arrow from the early sun,
she keeps losing track of the states. Indiana? Ohio?
Could this dreary stretch be Illinois? She doesn't know
where they're going and doesn't care because he has promised
horses and a long school-less afternoon. The two-lane road
is flanked by fields as far as her eyes will see. Occasionally
a tree cuts the view, fans out, flaming
its orange hues. Her hair tangles he's driving so fast.
She's not scared like her mother, always telling him,
Slow down!, fingers gone white from gripping the overhead
handhold, saying, There's no rush, we have time.
Time is something the girl doesn't know about,
not yet. Not for ten more years when her father will die
in a different car, trying to peel across the tracks
before a train. Tracks she'll have crossed safely
a hundred times. More. At this moment she only knows the wind
made fast and angry in a car with a single window,
no roof, only knows the fierce scent of stirred aftershave,
its fading. Later, she'll dream of an old man, liver-spotted,
loose-skinned. She'll see his calloused hands
twining wires in the engine of an old car, using parts
he's kept junking up the yard for years. He'll open
a gapped-toothed smile and tell her to get in,
they're going for a ride. He'll start up the Ford or Jeep
and drive them long hours into the wind.

AVERAGE

They tell her she was two, but she must have been older.
She knows too much. Knows the Louisville Slugger
splintering her lip. Running to her father. The four-inch
needle that tapped her tailbone. She was there. She has the scar to
prove it, the mass of tissue a tiny gold ball
in her lip. She can see that kid in the cotton play dress.
The grandparents' backyard. The towhead brother
at home plate. The green grass and blue sky. The easy, average
Midwestern afternoon. The perfect pitch.

DANIEL

He'd walked on water once in a neighbor's above-ground pool.
He was always under the influence of a misaligned sky.
He agreed one night and they had sex and never spoke of it again.
He always said pills were for girls and the razor up the wrist.
They'd spend the night in the thinning woods, tossing lit matches
into the Toledo dark.
The day Shannon had a second abortion the three of them
drank Boons until four in the morning.
He read everything he could to find out how to live.
He'd play guitar and they'd stare up at the breathless stars.
Fireflies would flame and fade.
Guns were for boys and men. Car exhaust in the garage,
the middle-aged woman's way.
When sneaking onto buildings he always trusted the scaffolding
would hold.
Tarred rooftops were too hot at noon.
He couldn't fathom the neck and a rope.
He believed before birth the soul chooses the thresholds and vice
grips ahead.
In this way traumas were not accidents.
You'll be beautiful, he said.

WHEN HER BROTHERS WERE BOYS

Snow excites
a young boy's eyes
with its skipping white.
Cold sweeps in,
freezing the pond
at Ottawa Park where long
after dark he skates
with his older brother,
who's shoveling snow
into a mound, clearing a rink.
The snow continues
to come down, draping the ice
in thin gauze. The boy
doesn't see the fissure, so rapt
in the motion of his legs,
scoring goals like Gretsky.
The air is cold.
His cheeks burn, a good burn
after days indoors,
waiting for the freeze.
He skates in circles,
slices to a stop,
pivots. He takes possession
of the puck, makes a clean
break toward the goal
among fans' cheers
and rivals' taunts so loud
he doesn't hear the snap
and crack, only feels
a leg slipping and water
seeping. He howls
from the cold. His brother
comes running, newly sharpened skates

fracturing the water more.
He dives from the pond
onto a snow bank
and watches the boy sink
to his chest. Later, his brother
will say he pulled him
to the shore with his stick. Later,
he'll say his lips were blue.
For three days the boy
coughed and shivered and couldn't
wiggle his toes. He dreamed
he had no legs. During the day
his brother sat on the cold porch
with the dog in the cold sun.
He willed snow to melt
and never wanted winter again.
At night he fed the boy boiled eggs
and broth. He sat by his bed,
touching hand to head
against the fever. *Please, I'll be good.*
The boy became well and stopped
dreaming he was Gretsky,
though he knew arena ice would hold
his weight. He tried football
and basketball. In the end,
he decided to run. Like so many
things then, he did this alone.
One summer he took her to the pond.
I heard the crack, he said. *I still hear it.*
He couldn't protect me then any more
than I can protect you now.

NORTHERN LIGHTS, FAIRBANKS, ALASKA

On the curving, gravel road
marked with snow, and beneath that,
ice, you
drove where dying trees thinned
and the peak,
flat tract of white,
met sky.
You weren't searching
for stars or the mocking curve
of the moon.
You weren't talking.
Time waited at the bottom,
on the lower road, the one that connects
to town. Earlier,
she'd said something
about pretending
and you took it seriously
enough to question every gesture
until that point. On the shoulder
small shrubs grown human
watched closely as you passed.
The few cabins were cold, quiet.
Pretending is something we all do
now and then. To act as if
is a way
to get through.
At the top
you kept inside the car.
The heater whispered to your feet,
and out the window
what you came all this way
to find wasn't there.

STAGES

1.

She's thinking of a place outside Toledo
where Erie rocks into a quiet cove
and teases a breakwall
where she and Shannon used to sit
drinking beer stolen from their fathers' refrigerators.
Piss warm by the time they reached the concrete pier.
They didn't like the taste but winced it down,
going for the loose view
of the moon and the rocky, watery
feeling that things in this world are okay.

2.

In Fairbanks, a valley
between rivers. Low rolling hills
at three horizons. Independence.
Light from everywhere steeping
everything with its off-white stroke
brilliant before winter.
And then winter.
The echoing snap of words.
Darkness. Always the dark to keep her
awake, the dark staring
down with its one eye.

3.

Three a.m. No rain.
Uncharacteristic heat keeps her
from dreaming. Soon Portland's sky
will give over to a cloudless panel of blue.
In Ohio, Shannon and her partner are
having a ceremony, and Texas
has revoked its law against sodomy,

which is something, which is nothing,
America has long been over.

IN THE MIDWEST EVERYONE IS KIND

Daniel's holding court late into the night
so in the moment he's the only moment
there is. He has such control, bending
others' minds on the back porch around
the warped mound of his own.
Telling them if God exists
he lives in the Midwest because
in the Midwest everyone is kind.
He lives in the long, shallow fields and small
towns at the ends of dirt roads where nothing
happens. That's what God does all day:
nothing. He's a still wind. Daniel's talk
moves from firefly ghosts gasping
for moisture in the air, to Daniel, still
talking, walking on water in the four-foot
above-ground pool. More talk of God
and life as a long, sometimes short, distraction
from death. She stares into the humid air,
inhaling its warm seltzer into her veins.
A smaller mind would feel at one with the world
on a night like this—muggy, in the midst
of friends, laughing, the mind loosened
of its traps, but she feels alone, as if
she's in the only head possible. Even
with Daniel she can't escape the heart's
hardening as another day comes on, spreading
over a stranger's acre of lawn.

NOSH

Your friends loiter in the backyard,
badminton rackets abandoned to the moist grass,
martini glasses now in pale hands.
A rare day of sun.
That morning you told her you were leaving.
You asked she keep together. Appearances for now,
no scenes. Your mind's made
like a sheet on a bed pulled crisply
to the head of the mattress.
All through the afternoon she keeps quiet.
She can't finish sentences. She looks at you
not seeing her. You haven't said her name
in eight hours. Her friends stay silent,
as if they, too, see your arms turn porcelain, foreign.
When she watches you gesture tightly, she knows
a year from now what she'll remember from this day
is the three o'clock sun, how it shined
against the ant-infested rind of a lemon.

OF ALL THE MARVELOUS THINGS

He'd stayed home
in the house, cooped,
bored, until he climbed
onto the kitchen counter
with a knife and opened
the cupboard in search of sugar.
Found instead, just that quick,
his head dripping blood.
He called down to the basement
where his sister was sneaking
cigarettes and calling boys.
She waved the stick around,
feeling brave, older. She talked
about teachers and cheerleading,
about the high school senior
she was going to get
to take her, a freshman,
to prom. When she inhaled
she inhaled right to the lungs.
I gotta go, she said,
dropping the phone
when she saw her brother,
bleeding. He'd just missed
his eye, and the head, it bleeds.
She stubbed the cigarette
into her jeans, pulled the sweatshirt
from her waist and wrapped it
like a turban around his head.
She called her parents
home from a friend's
house a mile away. Waiting outside
he crumpled to the ground.
Snow washed red

down into his clothes.
Lucky, they called him later, *blessed*,
and viewed the accident
gravely while his sister laughed
and lit a cigarette. As she saw it,
she'd caught hell for something
that had nothing at all
to do with luck and everything
to do with stupidity.

MADD RIVER, OHIO

When Daniel told her to jump, of course
she jumped. She couldn't be outdone.
There was that, and her own mind's call
to black, chancing broken bone, jumping
for the rush, the instant of losing, feeling.
She didn't know how deep she'd dropped
until she came gasping for air, breaking
the surface to emerge, her half-hardened heart
thumping against the cage of her chest.
For years, she'd wake repeatedly from dreams
of water, lagoons spilling out to sea, rain
flooding the streets of small cities, and that very river,
when she was fifteen, that welcomed her
from the height of forty-five feet. She'd looked
down at the muddy stillness while the wind
took swipes at her ears. At her side was Daniel,
swinging a leg over, *The great thing about water*,
he said, *it always makes room.*

RESOLUTION

Summers were one thing,
swimming a half mile through muddy
water to the raft with Daniel.
Always Daniel, who was most at home
in the blinding sun, who
would hate this weather, rain
all around. She keeps asking,
*How do I know if he was good
if he died young?*
A kind of night has come on, and
sitting in the idle air,
she's thinking this is nothing
of what she imagined.
This quietness. That acre of rain.
The long thoughts
she doesn't feel compelled to finish.
The sky is dark and keeping secrets.
She has decided she won't go back
to the Midwest and that city
that boasts amateur baseball
and an actor from the cast of M*A*S*H*
Won't go back to her brothers
and the other boys she knew,
older now, married, moved
to Michigan, raising boys of their own.
But Daniel she returns to
like an old song whose words
come back in the wrong order.
When she's this still, it seems impossible
that she's growing old. She sucks at a corner
of her lip where a knot of tissue
holds and wonders what else there
is to know of solitude

and connection than two people
lying side by side on a raft
in the sun. What else?
She tells herself she won't cry
for him again, knowing the tears
all along have been misplaced.

TREADING

She has been watching sparrows nest
beneath an eave. She thinks they're
sparrows but can't be sure. It's not
the red wine or smoke reddening lines
in the whites of her eyes. She hasn't taken
time to learn the names of these few things.
The neighbor's cat has killed another bird
and the remaining ones are gathering
in a dense matting of twig, wool, and feathers
of other birds. The mother, in a few days,
will fly to a nearby tree. The fledglings
will long for her and finally follow,
treading into their own patterns of flight.
She saw this last year when she'd tried
to quit smoking and had a week of the same dream:
she was in a room without windows
there wasn't a door
there was an opening of which she knew nothing

PORTRAIT OF THE UNSPOKEN

In from her evening walk, she found you
asleep near the rusted radiator. No blanket,
no sweatshirt, just your pale arms folded into infinity.
She'd come in from the woods behind the rented house
you felt you owned you'd been there that long,
repaired so much.

Out in those woods a girl, maybe eight,
was poking at banana slugs with a stick,
playing alone, playing at visibility,
her brother, four years dead, was more visible.

She doesn't remember slugs in Ohio, but burning
ants with a stream of sun through her glasses. She had
to squint away the light and squint to see the frenzied black
specks circling an invisible labyrinth.

She wanted to tell you a few things,
but you were curled in the distance, the reprieve,
of a sleep that would change everything. She didn't wake you.
She didn't bring you back to the skin
sliding from tender bones and your mother not-knowing
who you are. She didn't bring you back
to the frozen pea in your breast,
the one neither of you wanted to feel.

What she wanted to say was
the ground is wet and gives,
the girl was singing, and though out of season
a white heather has bloomed.

CULT OF MEMORY

> *I carried on a day-by-day story, which was*
> *the realest thing in my life.*
> —Eleanor Roosevelt

In the photo above the lamp, she's a child
sitting on her mother's lap as she reads a story

she no longer remembers. Their faces stare down
into the words. She has this photograph

but can't scare up the afternoon, where her siblings were,
which house they lived in. This lack of detail

feels like limbo, that region that borders hell.
For without a structured sense of her past,

she believes her future will be false.
She's troubled by something else:

if she had concrete memories, they wouldn't be
of her – whole, separate – but only her thoughts

of her, that time. Merely recollection of the mind's activity.
Her mother, in the photograph, is smoking. Wispy white curls

crowd the air above their faces.
Her canvas shoes are touched with mud.

She has no idea how either of them felt, who wanted whom
to read the story, if this was a rare occurrence.

No symptoms have surfaced, opening tunnels
to buried traumas, which might explain the white holes

in her memory. She tries to see through the long gaps
and fails to know who she was as a child or what

she wanted, so she begins to make it up: she was an only child.
Her father was a racecar driver. Her mother didn't work.

The story they were reading, because they read it
so often, is one she knows by heart.

PLEASURES

There are the usual and not so usual
pleasures. The elegant feet of a woman
she has recently met. The few round tomatoes
from her garden. Mexican girls shyly asking
money for the run for the arts.
Traffic pulling to the curb
as an ambulance wails. The long life ahead,
the lives left behind. Her mother
finally not questioning her every gesture.
A week not thinking her own death
is coming soon. And finally, after years,
her whole hand crushed by the trusting
muscles of the woman with the elegant feet.

WHAT HAS HAPPENED

Noon on a Saturday between Christmas and New Year's.
Around her is an unbroken panel of gray. The hills roll secretly
through the city and the dog that's usually barking isn't. On a day
like this she could drive through the damp and beaten streets,
eating an apple and snapping channels on the radio, stopping
only in front of a house where she used to live, where a light is on
and a woman is inside reading, where outside on the left,
the blackberry has grown angry and claws at the window.
Its thick vines months before disappeared into the earth,
tunneling taut arms beneath the house. The reasons
of the blackberry are simple and the same as the reasons
of the heart: wanting only to extend and cling. That she merely
had to walk out the back door or stretch a pale arm through
the window and pull a dulling black oval from the shrub's
unfailing ambition wasn't reason enough. On a day like this she
could stop off at the corner where the woman still buys cigarettes
and crack the lip of a beer and drive and drink, wedging the can
in the V of her legs. Heat could blow up the cuff of her jeans and
her skin prickle before flushing with warmth. The radio would
play unfamiliar songs while she thinks of that woman alone, or not
alone, and her in this car, beating a fist on the dash at each
memory of betrayal: so much silence, caressing the cats
instead of each other, nights out with a coworker until four
in the morning. She's driving in and out of the past and present,
thinking of the thousand drupelets staining the lawn, hoping
she won't repeat a goddamned thing.

THE ART OF FLYING

> ...*Cigarettes are the only way*
> *to make bleakness nutritional, or at least useful,*
> *something to do while terrified.*
> —B.H. FAIRCHILD, The Art of the Lathe

1.

The problem is you can't smoke on airplanes,
crammed in economy seats on cross-country
flights, five hours and only one shitty movie
to cut the recycled air and the odd
odors of fellow passengers resurrected with each
new bout of turbulence.

Nor in hospital rooms, after your first born
has smashed his moped and skidded his lean,
pale body across a rough stretch of pavement.
Nor at films based on Stephen King books.
How pleasing to light up in a dark theatre,
exhale quiet gray clouds, buffer to any celluloid terror.

2.

As if it were a lucky coin, or talisman,
she flips the butt of the one last
smoked. Lip end heads, ash end tails.
She can't take bets because the small white
cylinder can't keep balance and lands
on its side. At forty thousand feet, cruising,
she gets an idea and begins to suck
the unlit stub. She waits for the attendant
to draw attention to this basic need, oral, Freudian,
in its many functions. What will that do, but
draw from behind the posturing calm
the deadly crave masking the terrible fear

aching through everyone's body?
Really, she thinks, is it all that bad, being
forced to defer that long, thoughtful drag, the fullness
of smoke in the lungs, defer the arrowed exhale
shooting into a dark or light sky?

Yes.

She wants to be done with it. Wants the gratification,
wants to strike a match and smoke the pack.
Just for now, this moment, to tide her over
and keep her from thinking crashing thoughts.

NOTES TOWARD FLIGHT

She dreams her father is on the roof of a house. He wants to jump
to another roof because, he yells from up there, he has not taken
risks in his life. He paces back a few feet, runs to the edge, stops,
repeats this, makes it past the edge, but is still holding on.
He's caught mid-motion, a barrel-chested bird, mid-flight before
descent.

*

They're camped out beneath an afghan on the living room floor.
His bear huge body behind hers, the smell of Coca-cola, sweat,
beer. *We're camping out, kid, kid, do ya see the stars?*

*

He plays solitaire at the dark-drained oval table. The one she
polishes every Thanksgiving. She wedges between his arms, lap,
and the table's edge. She slips the cards, puts the aces in a row,
wins the one player game being played by two.

*

They wrestle on the floor. Two-hundred forty pounds on all fours.
Sixty-five of bone and muscle leaping through air swooped down
and taken in a thick-fingered tickle.

*

She's on the roof, square and forty stories up. She walks to a
corner, sprints diagonal to the other corner, jumps
       into the wind

HERE

In the first evening of rain announcing winter's advance,
her hands drop dry and delicate fibers into the crease
of thin paper. Her fingers roll tobacco into a small cylinder.

Behind her lights in the house are out and through a window,
she exhales into the downpour. Smoke swirls and disappears,
beaten by incessant lines of rain. She hears the cart and wet

cough of the woman gathering bottles and cans. In the dampness
and the dark, she has a vision of lungs opening with the invasion
of clean, irrefutable air. And in this moment, she wonders

what all the small constrictions that structure our memories
will amount to. She counts the empty tally, wishing for lightning,
hearing instead the faint crash of bottle against bottle against
bottle.

DANIEL

More and more her memories are misleading.
She worries about that. This morning
she was picturing his mouth moving, his lips.
Don't part your legs for just any smile.
The same trains keep passing.
Think of your skin in the summer when you get sad.
Dear Daniel dead now twenty years
won't leave her. *Don't do anything*
when you're lonely. We do everything
because we're lonely. We talk to ghosts.
Talking death doesn't seem so deep now, does it?
A bookend to the little you've done.
What's misleading is that none of this is
about the mouth exactly. It's the chest.
The breath. She wanted the goddamned breath
of that beautiful boy who hadn't yet grown
hair on his chest. *Don't wait around for people*
to tell you who they are, he's saying, *it all comes down*
to what the wind is doing to the neighbor's chimes.

TAG

You must not have gotten the message.
She wasn't planning on not coming
until it was too late to call a taxi,
what with the snow downing itself
and the sky (the sky is always to blame)
steeling over. You must have wondered
where she was. She did regret letting go the time,
but the tree from the kitchen window
held the white of the moon. You would
have liked the look. Seeing it, she thought of
some words for all that passed
between you. That's why she called from
the Texaco where the fluorescent light
made everything seem clearer. She says
it's your turn to say something about the missing
lamppost. It was an accident, though knowing
you, you'll call it something else.

QUANTUM THEORY

> *It would be nice if sometime a man would come up to
> me on the street and say, "Hello, I'm the information man, and
> you have not said the word 'yours' in thirteen minutes. You have
> not said the word 'praise' for eighteen days, three hours, and
> nineteen minutes."*
>
> —EDWARD RUSCHA, Information Man

What else has she not done? She has not
showered in four days. Not
called her mother or thought of her in ten.
She has not stopped on the path from her car
to her apartment to listen to the cold
creak of birches. She has not
been to church in three years, sixty-two days,
four hours. She has not observed a holiday this year.
She has not touched your lower back to draw you near.
She has not touched herself. She has never said
the word obsequious, nor considered that she has
wasted her life. She has not
called, but waited. She has waited and not been drunk
for eight hours, nor tasted fresh snow.

MIDLIFE

In the early hours of the black morning, before the streets
light with cars and noise, before workers wake and dress,
a plume of smoke drifts from a bedroom window.

Awake at an odd hour, she's studying the moon,
white comma in the night not flanked by word, only space.
The moon hangs unaided, worried that it has no place.

SYLVIA HOTEL

The shift began on the fifth
floor in a room where she could not
see the bay from the windows. Before that,
when she should have told you
the dead aren't due back,
ever. Looking down she saw ivy
climbing for the ledge. Outside
warm, slow breath met the wintering
air. And in the gray gloaming, she
saw the peach heat of your raised
torso and gazed dumbly as you explained,
to avoid stings, keep gentle bees.

JUG'S TAVERN

The sun covers the city in yellow
light, but it doesn't make its way
into the basement tavern, where paneled
walls keep white-trousered workers
from the ice cream factory and a few
stragglers from the Jeep plant farther
up the road. It doesn't matter
what day it is, the workday's done.
The whiskey bottle's ready.
The beer is cold. The bartender
has a cigarette perched like a bookie's
pencil behind his ear and as he bends
the cap on another bottle, he wonders
what it says about his life
that he serves these lives. Just
as quickly the thought is gone.
He resumes watching
the golden High Life
sweat its cold and ring
the counter with condensation.
In a booth is a girl reading a book
near the jaundiced light of a jukebox.
She has lived nearby her whole life, signed on
for the summer, saving her money
to take her past the flat land and out
where the sky isn't all there is.
In the basement bar, she's waiting
the while it takes for the regulars
to settle in, for the talking to begin.
> *There was another kid*
> *used to come in here, said the drinks*
> *were good and cheap. Summer help, too.*
> *Liked to drink. Busted up a gas station one night.*

Beat up a girl.
She's alone but doesn't mind. She imagines
her father coming to a place like this, talking up
an old car he was going to fix. About the hour
when the secrets of their secret lives come out,
she tucks her book away and listens:
I was gonna be a fireman
I was gonna sail around, down to Mexico
He didn't want kids; he didn't want nothing
I didn't know; I'm just doing what I'm doing
She knows she's one of them. One day
she'll be in another bar and think back to this age,
her whole life opening.
Don't stay on, kid. They'll ask you to stay on.
Offer benefits, the union. Whatever you're
dreaming over there, hold on to that,
don't be fooled.
She says nothing. Her head full
of a thousand secrets she doesn't
feel compelled to share.
For this summer, she'll come to the bar,
though it's not the coming she likes,
it's the leaving,
walking out the door
when the afternoon
has given way to evening
and the cool wind
carries her on.

HER MOTHER AND A MAN

After they've made love in the wizened light
of evening, the woman pulls her hair
into a bun and begins again rolling out the dough.

The man, on the back stoop, rolls a cigarette,
tempering the tobacco with thin curls
of marijuana. The horizon is a broken orange over the ocean.

He likes to visit the woman because she lives alone,
along a secluded stretch of beach and she touches
him carefully, like a nurse would a burn victim.

They met when the man had a habit of long walks
covering the same strip of sand near the woman's aging house.
She'd spent hours listening to his gentle voice

spin the regrets in his life: two fast marriages,
missing the birth of his only son, a fondness for whiskey.
Distance. His regrets are not unlike her own, moving

from Ohio after her husband died, leaving her children
alone to score bruises in their hearts and find
their own troubled roads through solitude and connection.

The woman, quiet in her kitchen, is thinking about the man's son
who three years ago inhaled the exhaust out of a rebuilt '67
Chevy. The man has told her he should have come home

early, he should have refused the rounds. He should have asked
more often, *How are you? Really.* All his evenings have the feel of
sunburned skin. He considers where in his life

he might have said *Yes.* He's in his sixties and having

November thoughts in June. The thick tide is coming in. She
knows he hates to watch it.

The dough rising in the oven, the woman looks out
at the man pushing smoke from his wrinkled lips. She thinks he
has a kind mouth. She thinks she will ask him not to come back.

THEATER ON DIVISION STREET

In the only open business at this hour
where the other undead gather
to watch strung out and sexed up

versions of themselves, on the milky screen
is the notion there are things to be endured.
And other's desires are no small things.

Two streets over from where she lives
a ransacked Cadillac rests on blocks.
She wanted to ask *how long? Was it for sale?*

By the looks of the house no one was home,
no one had been through for years.
If Daniel were here, he might find something

worth salvaging. A speaker or cushion.
He might pry the wreathed emblem from the hood.
Onscreen is the idea there's nobility in taking in all there is

and then more. At sixty-eight, her mother's
dating again, answering ads, blindly meeting the bodies
behind the text, their half-matched voices.

She can hear Daniel in all his dead wisdom:
People do this. They tie their scuffed-up shoes.
They fix their hair. They go out again into the night.

Onscreen is the notion you can get want you want.
In the theatre around her are people with dead wings.
She's not half her mother's age

and engaged in nothing less than self-endurance.

Outside in the courtyard hang abandoned pants
and two white shirts, useless flags in the roughest wind.

PARTICIPLING

She is sitting alone on the patio in the early morning. The sun
is crowning the back fence. She is remembering a photograph
on the wall of a diner, brightly lit, dirty. There was a woman
cradling a deformed man in a bathing pool. The photo was black
and white and soft, exact in its rendering of compassion. Exact
in ways her memory is not. In the diner she'd been arguing
with her mother about a man until finally she stopped trying
and watched the unmistakable care a waitress was taking
with a deaf man ordering toast. This was the dusty part of the day
in eastern Oregon. On her way home she stopped to watch
the expert execution of a double-play in a little league game
and two of the players sisters racing each other up the down
of a slide, hiding their secrets in the tunnel. After that day she
hated to move or speak, to spend words on useless things.
After that day she started thinking there are so many struggles one
could take up.

TAKING DOWN THE PLANE

When she was seventeen she climbed
into her dad's buggy and drove to the long
stretch of barbed fence where she parked
on a gravel shoulder and sat on the hood,
smoking stolen cigarettes and watching planes
take off and land. The outbound jumbos,
angry bulls on the runway, snorting, sneering,
as they groaned painfully toward her, now
standing barefoot, causing concave dimples
in the metal, yelling *Fuck you* and long
insensible syllables, yelling out her lungs,
her youth. The act felt so satisfying then, screaming
into the fake wind, exhausting her teenage body
until, falling back into the car, pulling the darkness
in, she'd feel invigorated.

Now, exhaustion finds her in the morning
at the alarm's insistent beep and throughout the day,
typing notes of a meeting at which she contributed little.
And on weekends when her time is her own
and she doesn't feel like doing a thing.
She doesn't want to consider that it's not exhaustion,
not the body's necessary collapse from a busy life,
but that it's boredom, or its sister, depression, coursing
through because she said no instead of yes,
because she left the Midwest in search of a life
less flat, and this can't possibly be it. What she does
consider is grabbing some Winstons, driving out
to the airport, finding a fence and a plane
and screaming into its deafening landing.

YOU DON'T NEED TO CATCH A THING

Her hand on your neck and the stray dog on the floor in the back.

Her mouth and an allegiance to witness every mundane thing, like the dead sparrow outside the Dairy Queen where there was no blood, but the form of a bird, one wing out, one tucked.

Her hunger, her indulgence. Smoking a cigarette, pouring herself out the window, into the wind.

Hollow is a word she has come to inhabit.
She remembers everything and she's still empty.

Waiting, some might say. Or was it wanting?

To the right the ocean pulls on the horizon.

She has this question that never leaves: What am I for? For you?
There have been no words for miles.

All at once she feels a burning down all around
where she can see her life
separate from the life she had when she left the Midwest.

She decides if she could be still she could be God.

Suddenly she asks you to tell her again about fishing.

You cast a wire into the water where it's moving.
Where the trout are. When you're out there,
the repetitive act of tossing a line in is enough.

ON FINDING SHE WAKES EARLIER AS SHE GETS OLDER

The see-tolees of thrushes, of course. But she has known
those camping: kind, repetitive warnings
moments before heat makes a prison of the tent.
The sky, then, indifferent as the sky now.
She'd call it older and thin, and needing to be smothered
with thick oils, but she knows that has nothing
to do with the sky. All that daydreaming, all that waiting,
pooled as expectation – for what? The more the years
gather behind her, the less certain she is. Yet she wakes early,
unintentionally, as if something wants her not to miss
what before she longed to sleep through: her head tangled
from wine or the sun bearing down on white sheets.
Or what she didn't want to sleep through: a lover
downstairs in a robe brewing coffee or thumbing stones
collected from beaches and snow banks. Outside the window,
the rustle of leaves foreshadows an afternoon's cool breeze. Early
it is still, and yes, too late.

THE NEW CHRONOLOGY

Today, snow in a place that never snows.

Today, she thinks all we have are moments that string together,
aging muscle fibers layered, pulling over joints,
drawing two parts close.

This small act repeated is what constitutes a life.

Yesterday she heard, *Keep lust the size of an elephant.*

She thought of a lover's words:
A week ago I couldn't pick your walk out of a crowd.

On days when tenderness fails, she considers
when she has reached without thought of consequence.

She coaches herself, *Don't hesitate.*

When she fails in this, too, she looks at the pink scar
from a chicken pock bloomed and lifted on the flesh
like the open face of a broken peony.

She learned early Descartes was wrong. To feel is to be,
though the sensation claims too much.

Everything becomes available at the near pace of immobility.

She imagines she will never know herself and soon
will see her face small and distorted in a nurse's eyes
as her kind hands massage the arthritic knuckles of a dying body.

EVERYTHING TO LOOK FORWARD TO

*The body contains the life
story just as much as the brain.*
—EDNA O'BRIEN

They suspended her mother's
bladder in a hammock
because the tissue around it
had gone slack, and she has taken
to wearing a dust mask when
she rides a bike, sometimes when she
works in the yard or merely stands
outside. You won't talk
to her those days. Only her eyes
show above the polyester
binding. Her eyes which she thinks
reveal too much as it is. Still,
you wait for the revelation
of lips before asking her to rub
your sore instep. It's true
you're both getting older
and have stopped telling each other
how beautiful you'll be
in your seventies. She tries not to notice
as she carries her body, which used to
carry her, through the day, or as she considers
a friend's mother who's having her
knees replaced with titanium.
They shave that big bone at an angle.
  The femur.
Yeah, they shave it.
She thinks of her father's face,
unshaven all her life.

DEAD LETTER OFFICE

Can you believe, fifty? Five instances of ten.
Golden. Freedom and new beginnings.
The saggiest balls and tits.
Leave it to me to dig at your maverick heart.
I've got my skyhooks embedded.
I'm always talking to you.
What do you have to say
    to me?
That I still need an audience.
That the whiskey's decimated my liver
and I'm too old for Boons.
Cigarettes are so unbecoming.
Why would any of that have changed?
The back porch has always been the only place to be.
Thrice divorced, smacking mosquitos with a wired racquet.
Bald. Wearing copper bracelets.
Making sculptures out of rusted metal.
Still reading everything.
Did you really see me converting
    to gratitude and playing at yoga?
The world continues to cling freakishly to particles.
The riotous soul will riot.
Would we still be friends?
In our way. I always knew I'd be one of many boys you'd love
in your stolid and shadow ways.
    Love and leave.
I know.
I left first.
But you and I go distances.
We've had lifetimes.
Don't worry. The earth keeps lapping the sun.
The delicate scaffolding holds.
You'll always hear my voice, its congested bark, broken devil on your shoulder,

Tilt the game!
Again, again.
You will be met with tentacles of lust
and the hummingbird's spastic dance.
My skyhooks
You feel them, right?
The drag and lift, the shake
until you break age-less into your own caustic trot.
Know this:
You have never been empty.
You are exactly as you should be.

AS SUMMER ENDS

Tonight, as summer ends
she's considering the shape
her hands have made
after caressing the bodies
of women she didn't know
she wouldn't see again. Sometimes
this looks like the roughened arc
of an ostrich egg. Other times
an orange five-pointed
columbine. When she looks
to the sky with its deep
pockets, she doesn't
expect an answer. For her
it's the dove white
sadness of all the world
in this one moment.
Though the sky has many points
to make, she'll go to bed
and fall will come.
And winter.
And she'll come in
from the first snow
and shape her hands
around the five points
of memory: the spine
in want or lip
in laughter, the distracted pull
on a four a.m. cigarette,
the thousand ways others' hands
have shaped her body. This
will allow dawn
to down itself over her, splitting
the night and blanching

her gray bones. This
will allow respite
through the long winter,
where she'll come to know,
absolutely, what she is.

PALIMPSEST

What she'll come to understand won't matter.
The repetitious sounds of traffic at daybreak
waking her, alone, will fill the space
she'd made for you. She thinks
thoughts now will sustain her like the sky
keeps still for the hummingbird. Yesterday
a different woman said one word: want.
She felt it when she said it and looked at her
and remembered the curve of your spine.
All our lives we layer in exactly this way the many
ideas that hold us. Today she imagined
a future in a cabin outside of town, snow
outside every window, and another woman inside.
Consoling thoughts come slowly, leave quickly.
She thinks about sustenance, the empty
fullness of the sky after rain. She has come to
understand the life she had with you was this same sky
burning out, a field that didn't stretch as far
as the eye could see, and this understanding,
though true, will fade into a fragile white, like the sky
having second thoughts in winter.

AS LONG AS YOU'RE HERE

She has been thinking of the inside
of your mouth. Red dawn opening
over a field of barley. A birch, its pale bark
crowded with the wasted words
of her youth. Long lanes of an aching
ocean and the cries of past lovers.
The swollen belly of a bitch in heat.
The thousand lives she hasn't lived.
There's also music rising
from the soft bow of your spine.
All of this is here.
She has been so lost.

THE BURDEN OF THE OPEN ROAD

Juniper reaches into the road
but she doesn't slow or swerve
and lets it scratch the glossy paint.
Her mind is on the place
in the desert where there's
an abandoned Jeep stripped
to delicate steel, and daily
being buried by sand.

Her father's steely eyes
would have seen the rusted, cracked frame
and then cylinder and shine.
He would have heard the pitch
wind makes buffeting the body.
He would have hauled it home,
and worked quietly, late
into the night, transforming the heavy,
wrecked metal into motion and speed.
Sunday he would take her out
to test his work. *I could drive for days*,
he'd say, listening to the smooth
shift from third to fourth, fourth
to an imaginary fifth. Straight
to California. 66 until it hits water.
Monday he would sell the car, sweep
the garage, start again.

He was always in the garage,
tinkering. *Your father's tinkering with some
new toy. Tell him to come in,
it's getting late.* She didn't see
his solitude as anything to wonder at.
Now she understands it was

his escape from a woman
he no longer loved, but couldn't
leave. People stayed in those days,
each morning forfeiting another
part of themselves. Even now
she couldn't guess what he really wanted.

It's Sunday. She's on a drive,
thinking how she's always leaving.
Late afternoon, the horizon blurs,
gray into yellow into blue.
She imagines not
having left for the simple idea
there might be others or other things.
She imagines not having left because she could.

The day he died her father took Sundays
with him. So she thought.
When the next one arrived,
she felt him, a passenger,
next to her, as she left school
and drove west
and kept driving
far out of the Midwest
past Wyoming sage and
Oregon brush until she reached
sand and water,
and lay her body down
for the first time to grieve
and rest.

It has become her habit
to take long drives on Sundays,
no one to see, nothing to say.
To drive out, get lost,

blow a tire or drop the clutch,
have someone
find her, put the car
away, someone who'll take
her arm, and say, *It's getting late.
Do you have somewhere to be?*

www.ingramcontent.com/pod-product-compliance
Lightning Source LLC
Chambersburg PA
CBHW030457010526
44118CB00011B/984